FABLES
& THEIR MORALS

ANDROCLES AND THE LION
to
THE FIELD OF TREASURE

by

Bruce and Becky Durost Fish

Chelsea House Publishers
Philadelphia

CHELSEA HOUSE PUBLISHERS
Editor in Chief Stephen Reginald
Managing Editor James D. Gallagher
Production Manager Pamela Loos
Art Director Sara Davis
Picture Editor Judy Hasday
Senior Production Editor Lisa Chippendale
Designers Takeshi Takahashi, Keith Trego

First Printing

1 3 5 7 9 8 6 4 2

Library of Congress Cataloging-in-Publication Data

Fish, Bruce.
Fables and their morals / by Bruce and Becky Durost Fish.
  p. cm.
Includes bibliographical references and index.
Summary: Illustrated retelling of one hundred classic fables
from around the world.

ISBN 0-7910-5210-9 (set), 0-7910-5211-7 (vol. 1),
0-7910-5212-5 (vol. 2), 0-7910-5213-3 (vol. 3),
0-7910-5214-1 (vol. 4)
1. Fables. 2. Tales. [1. Fables. 2. Folklore.] I. Fish, Becky
Durost. II. Title.
PZ8.2.F54Fab 1999   98–36355
398.2—dc21   CIP
                                                AC

CONTENTS

INTRODUCTION

Fables are stories that feature animals with human characteristics. The animals' experiences teach us lessons about life and the way people behave. The word *fable* comes from the Latin word *fabula*, which means "a telling." While the stories usually end with a moral that summarizes what the story is teaching, the emphasis is on the story itself.

Fables are one of the oldest forms of stories. Before it was easy to write things down, they were passed on orally. Parents or wise people in a village would tell the stories to the children, who would grow up and pass the stories on to their children. Originally fables were told as poems because it is easier to memorize words that rhyme and have rhythm than it is to remember prose.

One of the most famous fable writers was Aesop. Many people think he lived in or near Greece during the sixth century B.C. and created about 200 fables. As far as we know, Aesop never wrote down his fables. The first person known to have put Aesop's fables into a collection was Demetrius of Phaleron, who lived in the fourth century B.C.

Aesop's fables have remained popular for 2,600 years, making him one of the most successful figures in the history of literature. His stories spread throughout Greece and Rome. When the Roman Empire expanded as far as Britain, soldiers carried Aesop's stories with them all across what is now Europe. His stories even traveled to Japan. When Jesuit missionaries arrived in Japan during the 16th century, they taught Aesop's fables to the Japanese.

But Aesop's stories are not the only fables we know of from ancient times. Many scholars believe that fables in India date back to the fifth century B.C. They were first used to instruct followers of the Buddha about his teachings. Many of these early stories are called *Jakatas*. They are birth stories about the Buddha and tell some of his experiences when incarnated as different animals, that is, when he was born as various animals. These stories include morals.

Another important group of fables from India is called the *Pancatantra*. The *Pancatantra* was originally written in Sanskrit. The oldest copy of it available is an Arabic translation from the eighth century called the *Kalilah wa Dimnah*. The stories feature two jackals who counsel a lion king. The tales teach political wisdom and cunning. They were translated into many languages, and in the 13th century a Latin version reached Europe.

For centuries, China did not have fables because traditional Chinese thought did not accept the idea of animals thinking and behaving like humans. The Chinese preferred stories based on actual events. But between the fourth and sixth centuries, trade with India made Chinese Buddhists familiar with the Indian fables that helped explain Buddhist teachings. Chinese Buddhists adapted these fables and collected them in the book *Po-Yü ching*.

Japan also has a tradition of fables. Well before Aesop's fables reached Japan, the Japanese had official histories from the first and eighth centuries that featured stories about small, intelligent animals getting the better of big, stupid creatures.

Bernard Binlin Dadié, a 20th-century writer from the Ivory Coast, published several books of African fables and folktales that he collected from that continent's oral traditions. As in other regions of the world, African fables feature animals with human characteristics.

Because of the continuing popularity of fables, many authors have written their own collections. Some fables became quite long. These expanded stories are called *beast epics*. The most famous example of a beast epic is *Roman de*

Renart, written in the 12th century. It contains related stories about Renart the Fox, who represents a cunning man. But most fables are much shorter and in the style of Aesop.

The 12th century also produced a book of short fables by Marie de France, a French poet. Her book was called *Ysopets* and was very popular.

Another French poet, Jean de La Fontaine, published a 12-book collection of fables between 1668 and 1693. Titled *Fables,* these stories are among the greatest masterpieces of French literature. Some experts consider La Fontaine's fables to be the best ever written.

In the late 19th century, publishers began producing many more children's books. Because of this, more authors began using fables in their work. Lewis Carroll (whose real name was Charles Dodgson) released *Alice's Adventures in Wonderland* in 1865. Its animal characters such as the rabbit and the walrus have human qualities. Beatrix Potter self-published *The Tale of Peter Rabbit* in 1900. It was picked up by Frederick Warne and Company in 1902, and the collection of stories about Peter, his family, and Farmer McGregor became one of the best-selling children's books of all time.

Kenneth Grahame's *The Wind in the Willows* with its animal characters Mole, Rat, Badger, and Toad was published in 1908. And Christopher Robin's toy animal friends in *Winnie-the-Pooh* (1926) and *The House at Pooh Corner* (1928), by A. A. Milne, act like human beings and teach lessons about life.

In the 20th century, the use of fable took a darker turn with the publication in 1945 of George Orwell's *Animal Farm.* With the famous line "All animals are equal, but some animals are more equal than others," Orwell's story of animals in a farmyard pilloried Josef Stalin and his oppressive government in the U.S.S.R.

Watership Down, by Richard Adams, and *The Redwall Books,* by Brian Jacques, also draw on the fable tradition. Many science fiction fantasy books, such as J.R.R. Tolkien's

The Hobbit and *The Lord of the Rings* trilogy, use elements of the fable to give a greater sense of reality to the imaginary worlds where they take place.

As new means of storytelling have emerged, the fable has continued to be used effectively. Elements of the fable can be found in comic strips such as *Peanuts,* by Charles Schulz; *The Far Side,* by Gary Larson; and *Shoe,* by Jeff MacNelly. Movies such as *Babe* and *The Lion King* are fables presented through film.

Considering that fables have remained popular for thousands of years, it may only be a matter of time before they are adapted to computer games, virtual reality programs, and other creative avenues yet to be developed.

AESOP

Exactly who Aesop was remains a mystery. Some people think he never existed. They say that Aesop is a legendary figure who was invented to give a name to the anonymous creators of the roughly 200 fables that are attributed to him.

But from ancient times, people have told stories about Aesop and his life. Herodotus, a Greek historian who lived in the fifth century B.C., wrote that Aesop was a slave who lived in the sixth century B.C. Most other stories about Aesop agree that he was a sixth-century slave. One story says that his master Jadmon was so impressed with Aesop's wisdom that he freed the slave.

Stories differ about where Aesop was from. Some say that he was from Thrace, others that he was from Phrygia. An Egyptian biography written in the first century places Aesop as a slave on the island of Samos. Plutarch, a first-century Greek biographer, wrote that Aesop was an adviser to Croesus, the king of Lydia. While the places differ, they all are in or near what is now Greece and Turkey.

After Aesop was freed from slavery, stories tell of him traveling throughout the ancient world, advising rulers and telling stories to both teach and entertain. Some accounts say that Aesop went to the ancient kingdom of Babylon (modern Iran) and became a riddle solver for King Lycurgus.

Another story tells of Aesop visiting Athens and the court of its ruler Peisistratus. He convinced the citizens of Athens to keep Peisistratus as ruler by telling them the fable "The Frogs Who Wanted a King" (see volume 2 of this series).

A 14th-century monk named Maximus Planudes who

admired Aesop's fables described him as an ugly deformed dwarf. Earlier biographers don't mention Aesop's appearance. Many people think that if Aesop were so disfigured, people living closer to his time would have mentioned it.

Herodotus wrote that Aesop died in the Greek city of Delphi, an important religious center. Apparently the citizens became angry with Aesop and threw him off a cliff, but there are several differing accounts of what provoked their attack.

In one story, Croesus, the king of Lydia, sent Aesop as an ambassador to Delphi with a large sum of gold to distribute among the citizens. When Aesop arrived, he was so appalled by the citizens' greed that he refused to give them the gold. Instead he sent the money back to Croesus.

Another writer claims that the people of Delphi were offended by the sarcastic tone of Aesop's fables. Still others suggest that Aesop died as a punishment for embezzling money from Croesus or for stealing a silver cup.

Whatever the truth may be about Aesop's life and death, his stories continue to entertain and enlighten new generations of readers.

ANDROCLES AND THE LION

any years ago, a slave named Androcles escaped from the estate of his master and fled north into the forest.

One day, he heard a strange sound coming from the edge of a grass-filled meadow dotted with wildflowers. There, a large lion with a magnificent golden mane was lying on his side, moaning.

Androcles saw fresh blood oozing out around a large thorn in the lion's paw. He crept up to the beast and knelt down next to him. Holding his breath, Androcles pulled the thorn out, then washed the wound and wrapped it with a clean cloth. After the wound was bandaged, the lion began to gently lick Androcles' hands.

When many men crashed through the undergrowth around the meadow, the lion bounded away along a narrow path through the trees. Androcles sprinted down a trail in the underbrush, only to be trapped in a cleverly hidden net.

He was returned to his master, who sentenced him to be torn apart by wild animals.

Androcles was led out into an arena, where an enormous lion waited. The lion gave a mighty roar and charged, but then he knocked Androcles gently to the ground and began licking his face. Androcles felt the soft scratching wetness of the lion's tongue and recognized him as the creature from the forest.

Androcles' master approached them and was so moved when the slave told his story that he set both of them free.

Moral: Gratitude is the sign of a noble heart.

The Ants and the Grasshoppers

ll summer, the grasshoppers played and sang in the warm sunshine. They gave no thought to storing food for the coming winter or to finding warm places to live. Occasionally they came upon groups of ants, busy collecting food or moving dirt and stones out of the great gray mound of their colony home. The ants looked up at the grasshoppers and warned them against the coming winter.

But the grasshoppers only laughed and said, "You live too close to the ground to see the glories of the sky and the sun and the wind. Life for you is all work, for us it is all joy."

As summer turned to fall, the cold winds and rain of late October drove the grasshoppers from their favorite summer places. When hunger began to gnaw at them, they asked the ants for help.

The leaders of the ant colony listened patiently to the

grasshoppers' plight and then asked, "What did you do during the summer and the early fall?"

"Why, we sang and danced and laughed and toasted one another with spring water," the grasshoppers replied.

"But you ignored our warnings about the cold months," the ants reminded them. "You made fun of us for working and said we were missing out on the joys of life. You ridiculed us as clumsy dancers and acted superior because we couldn't fly. Perhaps a winter of cold and hunger will teach you the joys of hard work."

Moral: It is best to prepare long in advance for days of great need.

THE APE AND
THE FOX

ong ago, in a far off land of sun, rolling grasslands, and dark forests, there lived an ape who
was desperately unhappy. He had many good
things to eat, and a great river flowed through
the forest and out into the grasslands to quench his thirst.
Many tall treetops at the edge of the forest provided him
with shelter.

But he suffered from one great affliction. He had no tail.
Naturally, from the moment the ape had first opened his
eyes, he had been fascinated by tails.

He watched the lions parading about the grasslands, their
tails straight up in the air. He saw the zebras munching grass
in the hot sun and keeping a cloud of flies at bay with a swift
snap of their tails. Even his friends the monkeys had tails,
and they could swing through the trees much more easily
than he.

One day a fox passed through the forest, and the ape marveled at his bushy tail, all red, white, and gray.

He called out, "Sir Fox, your tail is so long and thick and magnificent, couldn't I have the use of some small part of it to adorn myself?"

The fox replied, "Since you are so anxious to have a tail, just think how terrible it would be for me to lose even a small part of mine."

Moral: Nature has designed each creature to fulfill its own role in the world. An ape with a tail would be as silly as a fox without one.

The Archer and the Lion

n archer went hunting in the forest and killed many animals with his powerful longbow. Soon, every animal fled at the mere rumor of his approach except the lion, who vowed to stop the archer's wicked deeds.

He smelled the man at a great distance and snuck near him, staying just out of sight. The archer sensed something following him and climbed up out of the trees onto a bare hillside to survey the land.

The lion circled around above the man, until he was hidden only 100 yards away. The archer looked down the slope, toward the undergrowth below him.

The lion charged out of the tree line. Before the beast had covered more than 25 yards, the archer jumped up, turned, and released an arrow.

The arrow buried itself in the lion's left shoulder, and he fell on the rock-strewn slope. He heaved himself up onto

three legs and staggered behind a line of boulders near the forest edge.

The archer called, "Show yourself, coward! I have the perfect place for your head among the other trophies in the great hall of my lodge."

A fox, who had watched the lion's attack, shouted encouragement, "Surely your strength can defeat this puny man."

The lion growled in frustration, "I cannot defeat an enemy who can strike me down without laying a hand on me." He limped off into the trees, and for the rest of his long life he avoided the sight, sound, and smell of men.

Moral: Beware of those who can strike at you from a distance.

THE BEES AND
THEIR MASTER

young man grew up in a family who raised bees that produced many different kinds of honey. After his parents retired to a nearby town, the man inherited the honey farm.

One day, the beekeeper needed to go into town for supplies. He locked the barn, the storage buildings, and the house. Next he checked on the hives, bid the bees farewell, and took off toward town.

A thief who had moved into that area was watching the beekeeper's farm from a grove of trees on the far side of the fields. Once the beekeeper left, the thief quickly approached the farm but found everything securely locked.

In great frustration, he began looking outside for anything of value. He soon found the hives and discovered that all the bees were out collecting nectar.

This looks like easy money, he thought.

The thief knocked the hives over and gathered up all the honeycombs he could carry.

When the beekeeper returned, he found the mangled remains of the hives. For the rest of the afternoon, he worked to repair them.

At sunset, the bees returned and were shocked to find their homes in such a state. They buzzed angrily around the beekeeper, stinging him several times.

The beekeeper shouted, "You ungrateful creatures. You failed to defend your hives from a thief, and now you attack me as I'm trying to repair them."

Moral: It's easy to confuse friends with enemies and do great harm to those who care for us.

THE BOASTING
MULE

here was once a mule who belonged to a farmer with a deep love for animals. He fed the mule the best-quality hay and oats, brushed him regularly, and made sure he had plenty of clean water to drink. On cold days he covered the animal with a thick blanket. When the weather was wet or snowy, he brought all his animals into a large barn that was warm and dry.

He asked the mule only to pull a small cart so the children in the family could go for rides around the farm.

Sometimes, the mule's good fortune made him very boastful. He would tell fantastic stories about his parents. "I'm sure my father was an Arabian and my mother was probably a registered quarter horse. There may even be some Clydesdale in my lineage. That's why the farmer has me pulling that cart."

A few years later, the farmer was forced to sell most of his animals. The mule's new owner mistreated his animals.

The mule's new home was a rough lean-to in the corner of a weed-infested pasture. It was hot during the day, cold at night, and gave little protection from wind or rain.

The mule pulled a plow all day, and at night he ate stale hay and drank water with green scum on it.

When asked about his lineage, he said, "My father must have been a donkey."

Moral: A rich fool raised in humble circumstances is ashamed of nothing so much as his own parents.

THE CAT AND
THE BIRDS

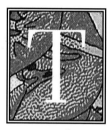he owners of a very large black-and-white cat named Oreo discovered he was badly overweight. They began to carefully measure the portions of food they fed him. The cat became hungry and wandered around the house meowing piteously. His owners banished Oreo from the house.

The cat prowled the neighborhood during the day, looking for food. At night he slept in the garage.

One day he overheard a conversation among a group of birds noisily eating thistle seed in a large cage. They were worried about a deadly new bird disease.

Oreo returned to the garage that night and quietly rummaged about in the boxes stored there. He found an old hat, a worn overcoat, a walking stick, and an empty bottle of cough syrup. He pushed these items out through his cat door and hid them.

The next day, he put on the hat and overcoat. He learned

to walk on his hind legs, carrying the walking stick in one paw and the medicine bottle in the other.

Later, Oreo approached the birdcage and called out to the birds. "Let me introduce myself. My name is Doctor Katzenschwartz, and I have some medicine here that will protect you from that sickness you've heard about."

The birds weren't fooled for a moment. "We all feel very well," they chirped, "and we'll remain that way as long as we're in here and you're out there."

Moral: Some who offer us help have their interests, not ours, in mind.

THE CAT AND
THE FOX

cat and a fox went walking in the woods on a warm summer's day. They discussed how their lives were similar and ways in which they were very different. The discussion turned to how they escaped from packs of hunting dogs and the humans who followed them for sport.

"I must confess," the cat began, "I have only one trick for eluding pursuit."

"What!" exclaimed the fox before the cat could finish. "Then how have you managed to live so long? I have many ways to escape from humans and their dogs. I can use my great speed to outdistance them, or I may plunge into the nearest stream to cover my scent. Climbing down a rocky cliff usually leaves them too frightened to follow."

Just then, they heard the loud baying of a pack of bloodhounds approaching.

"Here is my trick," cried the cat, as it raced up a tall tree and hid among the branches. "Now, show me yours."

From his vantage point, the cat saw the fox dart away at full speed, leaving the hounds far behind. Soon the fox plunged into a fast-flowing stream and then bounded toward a steep cliff face where the stream became a waterfall. At the bottom of the rocky slope, the fox stopped in front of a dense tree line.

Two dozen bloodhounds burst from the trees, surrounded the fox, and tore him to pieces.

Moral: One simple plan that works is worth more than many complex ones that fail.

THE CAT AND
THE MICE

One warm afternoon, the kitchen mice looked out their hole and across the floor to where a large gray cat lay in the sun.

One old mouse known for his wisdom exclaimed, "We have feared that creature for a long time, but today he is hardly breathing. How peaceful he looks. Have we been wrong to consider him such a dreadful menace?"

"Look how his fur glistens in the light," remarked another mouse. "It almost looks like our own. Perhaps mice and cats have a common ancestor."

"Whatever the truth of that," continued the older mouse, "it's clear that this cat is harmless at the moment. Let's collect some food from the kitchen pantry. There's no need to wait until nightfall and slink around like criminals."

The older mouse started across the floor in front of the cat, and many others followed. They had just reached the

pantry when the cat leaped toward them. The mice scattered, shrieking, and ran back toward their hole.

The old mouse had only covered half the distance to the hole when the cat grabbed him and began to bat him back and forth from one paw to the other.

"So, you think I am harmless," purred the cat, "and that we might even be related. Perhaps we should test this theory by becoming better acquainted."

The cat tossed the old mouse into the air, opened his mouth wide, and swallowed the creature in one horrible gulp.

Moral: A proven enemy will always remain a danger.

THE CAT AND THE
SPARROWS

A cat named Whiskers and two sparrows named Fleetwing and Hardbeak grew up in the same household and became great friends.

One day, the sparrows went out to explore while Whiskers napped on the windowsill. Soon the birds discovered a new suet feeder in a tree near their home.

Suddenly, a flock of starlings descended on the tree. Several rasping voices called out, "This is our tree now, our tree now, our tree now." Then they attacked the sparrows, who just managed to escape and fly home.

When Whiskers awoke, he found two bloody balls of feathers resting against his side. As he cleaned his friends up, they described the battle.

"We have to get rid of those birds," Whiskers said with quiet rage.

The three returned to the tree and found the starlings gorging themselves on suet.

"How dare you attack my friends," hissed the cat.

All the starlings screeched, "It's our tree now, our tree now, our tree now." Then they dove at the cat.

Whiskers slashed at the nearest bird with his claws, knocking it against the trunk of the tree and breaking its neck.

The joy of battle consumed him, and he continued killing for some time.

In the silence that followed, Whiskers found the sparrows lying unconscious near the tree. In the heat of the conflict, he had failed to distinguish friend from foe.

He picked them up gently, took them home, and nursed them back to health.

Moral: Passions that are aroused for our benefit may turn against us.

THE CAT, THE ROOSTER, AND THE YOUNG MOUSE

young mouse named Gregory grew up in a large, snug home behind a hole in the parlor wall of a great mansion. He was born with an insatiable curiosity.

Gregory scrambled about within the walls of the mansion, looking out through every crack, crevice, and hole, to see what he could discover. Late at night, he explored the huge library, carrying heavy books up to the highest shelves and reading them by the light of the moon.

As he grew older, Gregory was allowed to venture farther from home. He spent long days crisscrossing the yard and fields around the old mansion and then returned home with wonderful stories and unending questions.

One day he returned early, sat silently during dinner, and ate very little. After the meal, his father asked, "What has stolen both your voice and your appetite?"

"I saw two creatures today," he began. "The first was

gentle and quiet, with a rich fur coat and great liquid eyes. The other had pieces of raw meat on its head and under its chin. It must have torn them from the body of some poor wretch it killed. I'll always remember its fiendish cry and the way its wild red eyes stared at me."

Gregory's father smiled. "The second creature you saw was a rooster. It looks and sounds fierce, but it's more likely to run from you than attack you. But the first one is another matter. That was a cat, and he wanted to eat you."

Moral: Appearances can be deceiving.

THE CROW AND
THE PITCHER

crow on a long journey had to cross a barren
land of juniper trees, bunch grass, and sage-
brush. He flew all day in the hot sun, trying to
reach the green slopes of the mountains in the
distance.

As daylight faded, exhaustion and thirst drove him to
look for water and shade in the unforgiving land below. To
his great relief, he spotted the stony, winding track of a narrow streambed. He followed it to a small group of trees near
a low rock outcropping on the east side of a long, gently
sloping hill.

Here, he thought, *I'm sure to find a safe place to roost for the
night and water to quench my thirst.*

He circled down slowly, buffeted by the rough afternoon
air rising from the hot ground. The crow landed in a tall
juniper tree and looked for water in the streambed, but he
saw only dust and rocks.

Cackling in dismay, he dropped down to the streambed. Just beyond it he saw a tall stone water jar. It was half full of water, but it had such a narrow neck that the crow couldn't reach any to drink.

Then he had an idea. He picked up a small stone with his beak and dropped it into the jar. The water level rose a tiny bit. He dropped in more stones, and soon the water rose high enough for him to drink his fill.

Moral: Necessity is the mother of invention.

THE CUCKOO, THE HEDGE SPARROW, AND THE OWL

There once was a cuckoo who was so lazy that she didn't want to bother making a nest for her eggs. Instead she laid her eggs in a fine nest built by a hedge sparrow. Then she flew off and spent her days eating and sunning herself.

The hedge sparrow was surprised to find her nest full of eggs, but she was too kindhearted to shove them out. Instead she kept the eggs warm and drove off snakes who would have liked nothing better than fresh eggs for dinner.

Eventually the eggs hatched. The baby cuckoos cried from hunger, so the hedge sparrow searched for worms and bugs that would make the hatchlings grow.

The day arrived when the babies were big enough to live on their own. Saying goodbye to the hedge sparrow, they took turns diving from the nest and going off to explore the world.

When the mother cuckoo learned that the baby birds

had flown away without looking for her, she sat down on a branch next to the wise owl and complained.

"Would you believe it?" exclaimed the cuckoo. "Those birds have flown off without so much as speaking to me, their own mother. Such ingratitude!"

"Silence," said the owl. "Don't expect from others that which you have not given yourself. Before you complain about the ingratitude of your young, be thankful to the hedge sparrow who cared for the children you abandoned."

Moral: Before you teach gratitude to others, learn to be grateful yourself.

THE DOG AND
THE CURS

In many villages when a strange dog passes through, the curs or stray dogs of the village will chase him, barking at his heels to drive the dog from town. They don't want any competition for the scraps of food they live on, so the sooner they can get any new dogs out of town, the happier they are.

One day, a particularly well-bred dog ambled into a strange village. Immediately, the curs attacked him. The dog understood that turning tail and running would simply encourage the curs to keep chasing him. So instead, he turned around and faced his attackers. He bared his teeth, laid back his ears, and growled deep in his throat. His fur raised, and he leaned back on his hind legs as if ready to spring at one of the curs.

For a moment, the curs stood motionless, uncertain what to do. They had never met a dog who stood up to them.

The well-bred dog refused to back down. He continued growling and glared at first one cur and then another.

Soon he discovered that one set of teeth was worth two pairs of heels, because the curs, seeing that he was determined to hold his ground, slunk away with their tails between their legs. Rather than being chased out of town, the well-bred dog was free to go about his business at his own pace.

Moral: Putting up with bad behavior often leads to more problems.

THE DOG AND
THE SHADOW

hungry dog saw a large juicy piece of meat hanging in the marketplace. It looked so tender and he was so hungry that he couldn't resist stealing it. Before anyone could notice what he was doing, he leaped up, grabbed the meat with his teeth, and ran away.

Some distance from the marketplace, he came to a stream. A footbridge spanned the water, so the dog decided to cross over the bridge.

Suddenly his eye was caught by the image of another dog with a large piece of meat. The hungry dog stopped and stared down into the clear water. Sure enough, there was another dog with a piece of meat that looked just as big and juicy as the piece the hungry dog himself had stolen.

That dog isn't any bigger than I am, the hungry dog thought. *If I took his meat, I would have two pieces. Then I wouldn't be hungry for a week or more.*

Quickly he snapped at the other dog's meat. To his horror, when he opened his mouth to grab the other piece of meat, his own juicy piece fell into the stream and sank to the bottom. The other dog's piece of meat also disappeared. Too late, the hungry dog realized that he had been looking at his reflection. He had been chasing a shadow and now had nothing to fill his empty stomach but dreams of what might have been.

Moral: Grasp the shadow and lose the substance.

The Dog in the Manger

A dog wanted a soft place to rest his head at night, so he made his bed on some hay in a manger. He arranged the hay until he had just the right amount in the right places to make himself perfectly comfortable. *Life,* he sighed to himself, *is wonderful.*

One night, a horse who was almost starving approached the barn. When he saw the manger full of hay, he trotted right over to it so that he could eat.

Up sprang the dog, growling and snarling. He jumped at the starving horse, driving him back into the yard. No matter how the horse pleaded, the dog would not let the poor animal touch any of the hay.

Finally the horse said, "Curses on you, you selfish dog! You don't eat the hay yourself, and you could always add more hay to your manger to replace what I ate. But in your

spite, you won't let those of us who need to eat the hay enjoy any of it."

The commotion in the barnyard woke up the farmer, and he raced from the farmhouse to find out what was going on. When he saw what the dog was doing to the poor horse, the farmer took the dog by the scruff of the neck and whipped him soundly.

Completely embarrassed and shamed, the dog ran off and was never heard from again.

Moral: Contemptible people won't let others use what they themselves cannot enjoy.

The Dogs and
the Hides

ome dogs famished with hunger saw some
cowhides soaking deep at the bottom of the
river. The tanner had put the hides there to
soften. Just the sight of them made the dogs
salivate. Nothing had ever looked so delectable as those
cowhides, but the hungry dogs could not reach them
because the water was too deep and swift.

The dogs discussed various ways to solve their problem.
They couldn't agree on any of the solutions each proposed.
Finally, one dog said, "Let's drink up the river. Then we
could walk on the river bottom to the hides and eat our fill."

The other dogs perked up when they heard this idea and
quickly agreed to try it. They lined up along the river bank
and lapped and lapped and lapped the water. Nothing
appeared to happen. The water seemed to flow as swiftly as
before, and as high as ever.

"Don't be discouraged," called out one of the dogs. "We must simply try harder."

So the dogs continued drinking. Some of them began to feel sick from drinking so much water. Suddenly one of the dogs burst because there was so much water in his stomach. One by one, his friends burst as well. None of the dogs survived, and the hides lay just as far away and just as deep in the water as when the dogs first saw them.

Moral: Those who try to do things in impossible ways are apt to ruin themselves in the attempt.

The Donkey and His Driver

A restless donkey was being driven along a high road. He was tired of always going wherever his driver directed. For once, he wanted to decide where to go. He wanted to control his own destiny.

Suddenly the donkey bolted and ran to the edge of a precipice. He looked down. Far below, he could see a silver strand where light reflected off a river. He had never seen a river from such a height before.

Just as the donkey was about to throw himself over the edge, his driver grabbed him by the tail. Straining as hard as he could, the driver tried to pull the donkey back from the edge. He yanked and tugged on the donkey's tail, digging his heels into the ground so that he would have better leverage. He shouted that if the donkey didn't move back, he would get killed.

The donkey ignored his driver completely. If anything, the animal worked harder to reach the edge of the precipice.

When the driver realized that he was in danger of getting dragged over the edge along with the donkey, he quit trying to save the animal.

"Well, Jack," he said to the donkey, "if you want to be master of your destiny, I cannot help it. You have conquered me, but your victory comes at a great cost."

As the driver let go of the donkey's tail, the animal fell to his death.

Moral: A stubborn and willful life is often short.

The Donkey and His Shadow

One extremely hot day, a man hired a donkey and his driver to carry him across a sandy plain. The sun beat down mercilessly, and the sands reflected it, making the heat unbearable. At last the man was so overcome by the heat that he had to take a rest.

"Driver," he called, "this heat is overwhelming. Let us stop and take a rest before we finish our journey."

The driver willingly pulled the donkey to a stop, and his passenger immediately sat down in the shadow of the donkey, seeking to gain some relief from the sun.

The driver rudely pushed the man aside and sat down in the shade himself.

"This is not right," the passenger protested. "I hired you to take me across the plain, so I should be able to use the donkey's shadow."

"Oh no, friend," said the driver. "When you hired this

donkey from me, you said nothing about wanting the use of his shadow as well. If you want to use his shadow now, you must pay for it."

"What nonsense is this?" asked the passenger. "The donkey's shadow comes with the donkey. You can't have one without the other."

The two men began arguing bitterly over who would get to sit in the donkey's shadow. As they bickered, the donkey took to his heels and ran off, taking his shadow with him. So neither man got to sit in the donkey's shadow.

Moral: For some people arguing is more important than life.

THE DONKEY AND
THE LION

lion agreed to go hunting with a donkey. Knowing that the donkey was not skilled at catching prey, the lion sent him into the forest to bray as hard as he could.

"Your braying," said the lion, "will rouse the beasts, and they will run out of the forest to get away from the noise. I will stand here and catch all the animals that run this way."

The donkey agreed to this plan and hid himself in a thicket in the forest. Then he made the most hideous sounds he was capable of producing. Soon the ground was shaking from the weight of stampeding animals running from the woods to escape the horrible hee-hawing.

Whenever the sounds of the animals died away, the donkey began to bray again, driving more beasts out of the woods. The hunt continued in this way well into the morning. When the lion finally tired of killing prey, he called the donkey out of the woods.

Eagerly the donkey counted all the animals the lion had killed. He had never seen so many destroyed in one hunt.

"Aren't I an excellent hunter?" asked the conceited donkey. "Look at all the prey we have. I'm sure you've never hunted with a more skilled partner. Didn't I do well?"

"Excellently well," said the lion sarcastically. "Had I not known you for a donkey, I should have been frightened myself."

Moral: Those who deserve the least credit frequently claim the most.

THE DONKEY
CARRYING THE IMAGE

The people of a certain city worked hard to collect enough money so that they could purchase a wooden image for one of their temples. After several months, they were able to pay an artisan to create the special image, and at last the day came when the image would be delivered.

The people planned a great celebration. Shops closed, and everyone dressed in their best clothing. The women of the city prepared special foods. Live music filled the air, and the entire city was ready to celebrate this wonderful event.

At noon, a hush fell over the city. It was time for the image to be carried to the temple. The people quietly lined the streets, waiting for the image to pass by.

A donkey and his driver had been hired to carry the image. As the donkey passed through the crowds lining the route to the temple, the people spoke reverently and bowed down to the ground.

The donkey thought the people were bowing to him. He stretched his neck and bristled with pride. He gave himself airs and refused to move when his driver asked him to.

The driver, seeing the donkey stalled in the middle of the road, snapped his whip across the donkey's shoulders. "Oh, you stubborn idiot!" he said. "We have not yet reached the point where people will worship a donkey. Now move if you know what is good for you."

Moral: Only fools steal the credit due others.

The Donkey
Eating Thistles

t harvest time, a man hired some reapers to help him bring in his crops. Instead of the workers tramping to the house to eat, the master had his donkey bring food for the noon meal out to him and the workers in the field. The master was a good man and always provided the best food and drink for his reapers. He offered them pure, cool spring water and food seasoned with fresh herbs. Just the smell of it made the men's mouths water.

One day as the donkey carried the noon meal out to the field, he spied a thistle by the side of the road. It reached higher than his nose and was covered with small thorns. Immediately he trotted over to the thistle and bit down on it hungrily. His mouth filled with bitter juice, but he did not mind. Soon he had eaten the entire thistle down to the ground, thorns and all.

Many people would wonder, he thought as he licked his

lips, *why I am not tempted to eat some of the savory food I carry on my back. But to me, nothing could taste better than this bitter and thorny thistle. If only I could eat thistles like this every day, how content I would be!*

Moral: What's a delicacy to one person is tasteless to the other. But those people who know what they like and are not embarrassed to admit it gain more joy from life than many of their neighbors.

THE DONKEY IN
THE LION'S SKIN

A donkey was wandering out in a field when he found a lion's skin that some hunters had left out in the sun to dry.

An idea struck him. *If I covered myself with this lion's skin, people would think I was a lion instead of a donkey,* he said to himself. *They would run when they saw me coming instead of making fun of me for being a stupid donkey.*

Looking around to make sure no one could see him, the donkey crawled underneath the lion's skin and stood up. He walked to a nearby pond and looked at his reflection. Sure enough, he no longer looked like a donkey.

Full of confidence, the donkey strode through the neighborhood, spreading terror wherever he was seen. Everyone was afraid that the lion would steal their sheep or attack their children.

The donkey's success did not last, however. His master, who knew the donkey well, saw the lion that everyone was

talking about and noticed something odd. Under the lion's mane were what looked like long ears. Then the donkey's master heard the lion's voice and recognized it as belonging to his donkey.

Angered at the fear the donkey had spread among his neighbors, the master grabbed a stout stick and beat the donkey. The donkey soon realized that, even draped in the glorious lion's skin, he wasn't a lion after all.

Moral: Fine clothes may disguise a person's true nature, but silly words will reveal a fool.

THE DOVE AND
THE CROW

young dove was captured and put in a cage. She received plenty of food and water, but she was not allowed to fly wherever she wanted as she had earlier in her life.

While she missed her freedom, she learned to accept the confines of her cage. She even made friends with a crow who would occasionally perch on the sill of the window in the room where her cage hung and bring her gossip from the larger world.

Eventually the captive dove laid some eggs. Patiently she sat on the eggs, turning them so that they would stay evenly warm.

The day came when the eggs hatched, and all the dove's chicks were healthy and full of energy. The dove counted her babies and was pleased to discover that she had half again as many children as most doves her age.

"Isn't this wonderful?" she said to her friend the crow

when he stopped by one day. "I have so many healthy young babies to care for. I don't know that I've ever heard of any other dove having such a large family."

The crow shook its head sadly. "Good soul," it said to the dove, "don't boast about how large your family is. You live in a cage and are not free. The more young ones you have, the more slaves you will have to groan over when they grow up and are taken from you."

Moral: What are blessings in freedom are curses in slavery.

THE FIELD
OF TREASURE

farmer was dying, and as he thought of all the things life had taught him, he knew one lesson was the most important to pass on to his sons.

So he called his sons together and said to them: "My sons, I am dying. All the treasure I have is yours; if you look you will find it hidden in the large field next to our home."

Within a few days, the farmer died. His sons loved him deeply and grieved over their loss. Soon, however, they realized they must search for the treasure their father had left them.

Not wanting to destroy anything of value, they carefully dug up the field from one end to the other. The sun beat hot on their shoulders. Sweat rolled down their faces. They became very tired, but they persisted in digging up the field. When they had turned over the last piece of earth, they looked at each other in dismay. They had found no treasure.

"Well," said one brother, "since we have gone to so much trouble, we might as well sow the field with corn."

The field was quickly planted, and in time the brothers harvested a crop five times richer than any crop planted in that field before. When the brothers saw the size of the harvest, they remembered their father's words and realized the hidden treasure was not in gold but in the results of honest work.

Moral: Diligence makes riches.

FURTHER READINGS

Caduto, Michael J. *Earth Tales from Around the World*. Golden, Colo.: Fulcrum, 1997.

Creedon, Sharon. *Fair is Fair: World Folktales of Justice*. Little Rock, Ark.: August House, 1997.

Czernecki, Stefan. *The Cricket's Cage: A Chinese Folktale*. New York: Hyperion, 1997.

Goble, Paul. *Iktomi and the Buzzard: A Plains Indian Story*. New York: Orchard, 1994.

Gonzalez, Lucia M. *The Bossy Gallito: A Traditional Cuban Folk Tale*. New York: Scholastic, 1994.

Han, Suzanne Crowder. *The Rabbit's Judgment*. New York: Holt, 1994.

London, Jonathan. *What Newt Could Do for Turtle*. Cambridge, Mass.: Candlewick, 1996.

Martin, Rafe ed. *Mysterious Tales of Japan*. New York: Putnam, 1996.

Mayo, Margaret. *When the World Was Young: Creation and Pourquois Tales*. New York: Simon & Schuster, 1996.

Reneaux, J. J. *Why Alligator Hates Dog: A Cajun Folktale*. Little Rock, Ark.: August House, 1995.

Ross, Gale. *How Turtle's Back Was Cracked: A Traditional Cherokee Tale*. New York: Dial, 1995.

Roth, Susan L. *The Biggest Frog in Australia*. New York: Simon & Schuster, 1996.

Voake, Charlotte. *Ginger*. Cambridge, Mass.: Candlewick, 1997.

Walking Turtle, Eagle. *Full Moon Stories: Thirteen Native American Legends*. New York: Hyperion, 1997.

Index

BRUCE and BECKY DUROST FISH are freelance writers and editors who have worked on more than one hundred books for children and young adults. They have degrees in history and literature and live in the high desert of Central Oregon.